BIRDS
of the
Sherborne Missal

Also by Elisabeth Bletsoe

The Regardians: a book of angels
Portraits of the Artist's Sister
Pharmacopœia & Selected Early Works *
Landscape from a Dream *

An asterisk denotes a Shearsman title.

Elisabeth Bletsoe

BIRDS
of the
Sherborne Missal

Shearsman Books

First published in the United Kingdom in 2021 by
Shearsman Books Ltd
PO Box 4239
Swindon
SN3 9FN

Shearsman Books Ltd Registered Office
30–31 St. James Place, Mangotsfield, Bristol BS16 9JB
(this address not for correspondence)

www.shearsman.com

ISBN 978-1-84861-748-3

For permission to reproduce images from the
Sherborne Missal (Additional MS 74236),
we are grateful to The British Library.

CONTENTS

Preface 7

PREFACE

A missal contains the text and often the music to conduct the Christian Mass throughout the year and the one at Sherborne was created c. 1400 for the monks of the Benedictine Abbey there. It is unique for its remarkable marginal series of naturalistic birds, most of which are native to the area and often given their dialect names. These are mainly to be found in the central pages, appropriately where there is also inscribed musical notation. The missal's lavish scale and decoration served to emphasise the town's spiritual pre-eminence in Wessex.

In this poem-cycle, each bird was observed in its native habitat within the boundaries of the Sherborne diocese and then linked back to the missal by means of religious iconography, imagery relating to books, pigments or methods of illumination as well as bird mythology, the latter often subverting the original Christian intention. The Japanese haibun was loosely employed as its form is well suited to nature-notes and the similar sized blocks of text were visually pleasing, echoing the blocks of heavy Gothic script. The accompanying haiku allowed for a brief word-sketch of the bird or its surroundings, which literally illuminated the whole.

These poems are a celebration of a unique Dorset landscape, made famous by its portrayal in Thomas Hardy's *The Woodlanders*. However, even during the two decades I have lived here, its fragility has become more apparent, with increasing loss of biodiversity and habitat due to unsympathetic developments and industrial-scale farming methods.

Provenance of the images included in this volume

Page Nº	Missal Page Nº
10	364
14	382
18	374
22	385
26	371
30	392
34	377
38	386
42	385
46	383
50	386
54	392
58	389, 372
62	369
66	368
70	382
74	374
78	363
82	373
86	368

Further Reading:

Janet Backhouse, *The Sherborne Missal*, London: The British Library, 1999.

Janet Backhouse, *Medieval Birds in the Sherborne Missal*, London: The British Library, 2001.

I.
Unnamed, identified as Goldfinch
(Carduelis carduelis)
for Suzanne

Days of brief transparency, viewed through a window of ice, lifted. Powdered across the lane. Having a porous cuttle texture as if drawn "using a thin & rather scratchy nib". A stricter regimen being currently observed, blood temporarily withdraws. Lenthay copse smokily obscure. Brittle scrapiness of reeds, bones packed tight with air. Fish-spine delicate. A tenebrous rustle, like the breathing of books. Fields growing nothing but stones, bone white, buff white, ivory white, carved by the river Yeo, formerly the Gifle or forked one. Abounding in small flocks among the alders; a *c'irm* or charm indicating a tinnitus of small bells, blended, a continual weaving of waters. Angel speaks with a multitudinous voice. "Thistle-tweaker", a conflation of thorns with the scarlet forehead becomes the iconography of crucifixion myth, ousting earlier fertile goddess affinities. Its nest a vaginal metaphor; a labyrinth of tender intricacies. *Lucina*, caged by the fingers of holy infants.

> sparkling up from
> the dried burdock heads, "a shrill
> piping of plenty"

II.
Roddok, Robin
(Erithacus rubecula)

Becoming secretive & depressed in the later months, before the vigorous reassertion of autumn territory. Stakes & ties. Paths of observance newly laid through contusions of aster, sedum and verbena *bonariensis*, helmeted with bees; offertories yielding a roman tessera, three pebbles from Chesil Bank & a tennis ball. A smell of burning moxa. Sulphur being ground with mercury to form vermilion; glazed with madder, sealed. Red as a releaser (your fat cherry lips), the impossible fury of it all. Oscillograph of the throat, that bob, bob, bobbing thing. Boundaries constructed from scribbles of sound. Marginals encompass the crossing at North Road, where fifteen burials "very shallow & without coffins" marked the putative site of Swithun's chapel. Haunter of low places & diggings, befitting associations with early resurrection cults. A bird so hallowed such that, harming it, the offending hand would forever uncontrollably tremble. Bringer of fire from the chthonian levels, that our lives might blaze inches from shadow; burnt feathers colour of bright fame. Covering the bodies of the dead with leaves.

> tweezing grey hairs
> in the bathroom; outside a robin's
> winter song

tibus

in om

eus. e

donis

sancti

III.
Unnamed, identified as Woodcock
(Scolopax rusticola)

Being considered as late as the eighteenth century that
they spent their months of absence on the moon, an
idea preferred to the risible new migration theory. The
declension from lunar pastures, a glissade down streams
of refrigerant light congealing while filtered through
earth's atmosphere. A millennial count of sixteen on the
Castle Estates recorded as "noteworthy". Frost-triggered,
tumbled by Siberian winds; a fall, falling. Into daylight
hours of trance-like stillness. Lines of infection tracing
the foundations of the derelict war hospital. The isolation
unit, brambled. Aggregates of hyphae form underground
cities of mycelia; endless ramifications, the deliquescence
of fruiting bodies. Earth pigments, superfine ochres, sepia
& sootblack in a complex marbling. Almost present, not
quite absent; *I am not here, I am something else.* Limned
in such manuscripts owing to the succulence of their
flesh; whole, roasted. Hepatic lobes of beefsteak polypore
exude a sanguineous juice; votive gifts pressed into bark
fissures: sheepwool, calcite chips, a palm cross, attended
by wasps. The pin-feather sought for its precision fineness
"to remove the mote from thy brother's eye"; mounted in
silver, to bring a woman to pleasure.

                    in my mind's
            eye, brooding; a heap of dead
            leaves on dead leaves

IV.
Stare, Starling
(Sturnus vulgaris)

Ring-angels on the radar testament to starling diaspora. From the Greek, *psaros*, spotted or flecked. Hand against sky leaking through fingers; the point where everything breaks through. Refractive famishings. Flight as a single-celled animal, a granular flow into pseudopodia, pushing towards fission & fusion. The twisting of nuclei form trace-memories of divinatory meaning. Pound Road; domed canopy of the Monterey cypress, gravid with song, counter-pointed by the five flute-towers of Lombardy poplar in Blacksmith's Lane. Sugar of hedge-fruits turning to alcohol. Rumours of adolescent sciamachy; the stoning of hanging baskets, toppling of garden urns. Attempted gun-sales at Pack Monday Fair; addicts buying lemons at local stores. The passage of saints-days in a watershine shatter of glass: Wulfsin & Aldhelm, Emerenciana & Juthware. Rough music, *charivari*. Ammoniac stench of the roost inviting various scatological nicknames. (Shitlegs). That petrol iridescence. A breast, "crowded with lustrous stars".

> blackberry theft;
> juveniles mimic Richard the
> cabbie's ring-tones

V.
Waysteter, Pied wagtail
(Motacilla alba)

Ambiguities of black and white. Delighting in even a small & temporary gathering of waters. In brief fugue through the osseous bird-cage of the monks' lavatorium; an emersion of helical patternings under the rain glaze on its blue liassic floor, star-creatures lost in chalk seas in primordial times. Elemental scratching; refusal of the public-school boys to tread its deep surface, architectural spaces infested with elegant & obsolete ritual. Ancestral games. A sylph-like buoyancy against the cohesive bulk of the abbey, internal voices transmitting its prescriptive fictions. Darkening ghosts pasted to the weighted song of the stone, damply. A conduit, to lead, but nowhere, of the emotions; lengths being taken to avoid extremes, the careful monitoring of lithium in the veins. Unwitting bride, squaring up to the lens under Bow Arch, place of rebel execution. A veil escaping in a stirring of winds; a bird in lovely & undulant motion. Carrying within, always, the leaven of instant flight, the announcing of wings.

running running   shaking off
three drops of devil's blood from the tail
                              tip

nus
mon
d nu
fiat i
sanp

VI.
Mew, Gull
(Larus argentatus)

Moving into the more solemn part of the Mass; gold foil running through the hedge, buffed by a wolf's tooth. Clifton Maubank, *Cliftune,* concealed by dark flickerings of holly-oak; the storm horizon. Walled about with a batteled wall & "sette with all sorts". With naked foot stalking in my chamber. Legendary ash plantings, the once ever-open door. The writhe of negotiations and giftings. Alluvial soils, prone to flood: in fallow waves bathing, broading out their feathers among small flowering crucifers crushed by the hooves of cattle. Lustral gatherings; the flock a lucent stillness, heart's needle fixed to the south-east. *Varium et mutabile,* the cupreous light. A driveway, chagrined by leaves, pinnate & palmate. Breaking within, stone by stone, piece by piece, the structures of desire; the sun's low deception. Resteth here, that quick could never rest, *laros,* the ravening ones, implacable spirits of the drowned. An absent finial, a tree hairy with virus. The last worst enemy, to face impermanence; sunlight flash in a seagull's wingpit.

> "Sea-gulls, winter mews,
> haunt the fallow.
> Beetles flie."

VII.

Sparwe, Sparrow
(Passer domesticus)
for Michell

Waiting for Sylvia, who never arrived. In back of *The Plume of Feathers*, a narrow sanctum in hibernal state, graced by the fluttering of small lives. Mimosa racemes. Roof-angles, at variance, drawn by the impetus of the abbey tower against ever finer & finer grindings of lapis & azurite. Into depthless sky. An insistent cheeping surpasses the bells' doxology; illicit couplings betrayed in a tremor of ivy. Naked stems of the winterstruck clematis proximate to the red bench; a simple narrative that becomes more complex; there is you, myself & many others like fingerprints among the lichen, staining. Faces that open & close. Things half-buried, annealed by frost. The inn a former mortuary, museum of autoptic secrets; no random event the disclosure of a statue of the risen Christ hidden within its walls. Sparrows gather, conductors of souls; only one human pair of eyes witnesses the child riding her trike across the flagstones. Back & forth, back & forth.

      high gothic letters
      blown by the wind; let sparrows
      make a nest of them

ne
thi
na

ꝑcpm̄

ꝙ

VIII.
Heyrun, Heron
(Ardea cinerea)

A page that encompasses the whole sky folds down to the shape of a heron, flying. Avian blood-cells a reliquary from cretaceous days; the serpentine throat, the gist of reptiles. Pterodactylar span devouring the land gifted by Athelstan as barter for the soul's yearly mass; to Aenna's Pool, the Coombe of the Pigsty, Ecgulf's Tree, Aetta's Dean, "for all time". Pastures garlanded with wire and electricity. Barbed & tanged. Bird flesh that waxes and wanes in lunar synchrony with the lady's smock, vacillatory cress-hordes at the margins of the parish water-meadow. *Fons limpidus.* River-ephemera gather at Smear's Bridge; pollen spicules, florets of eltrot, a meniscoid bulging. The circumspect gaze; irides chrome-yellow, orbits naked, livid. From the banks of the Yeo, a stone frieze of three Magi, one bearing apparently a head, severed. A boy bringing to school a heron killed while attempting to swallow a live vole; the children of Bradford Abbas being "deeply interested in this riverside tragedy".

water glancing light;

the long patience

A : Throstil cok

IX.
Throstil cok, male Blackbird
(Turdus merula)
for Ian

Desultory & melodious with more intricate phraseology
as the season advances; discarded notes upwardly forming
invisible rooms of ancillary miracles in which to inhabit/yet
to be built. Song-post on the Almshouse roof a nodal point
above the facial ruin of a luetic angel. Imperatives from the
Lamb & the Eagle. Reciting of Our Lady Psalter five times
daily in contemplation of death & judgement, a cloister of
swept shadows. Trendle Street, Westbury; abandoned on
unassuming corners, the simulacrum pertains. Teenagers
dressed in rags of birds crowd the doorway of Docherty's
Bar with aromas of batter & pea-wet. Distinctions elide
between male & female, dark & light: [overheard] *"I'm in
a state of flux right now".* Apprehensions of subcutaneous
violence like a distant bruise, a sky staining with orpiment.
Budding yeasty moon under poriferous cloud. A saint
opens a hand to find in his palm a small blue-green egg.
Words thicken, unimportant & unanswered. Only being
alive is left; the pulse, tic of raised tail-feathers on landing.
Sung for its own sake.

midnight alarm-calls:
last bird of evening or
    first of morning?

X.

Kyngynsfystere, Kingfisher
(Alcedo atthis)
for Andrew T.

River-babel is silence & intransigence, relinquished, becoming liquid. Interpretations manifest beyond the confines of a small group of trees. Glimpsed, a gift granted to only the righteous; low over the water, seeking its reconfigured ark. Mythologised chromatics: the banded demoiselle, ocellate wings of the peacock butterfly, the emperor's patrolling eye. Skimmers & chasers. A floating nest at once hollow & solid, hexatinellid structures crystallising outward. Crumbling in the hand, Aristotelian flim-flam, a fabrication from the spines of garfish. *Vire-vent*; dried & hung by its beak, the body would constantly turn, breasting the weather's direction. Wind-blown & touched by the fire. As though that vital spark survived still, through the agent of "mysterious energetic remains". At the surface, the piercing plunge into air, penetration of the aqueous envelope, reflexive sun augmented by an orrery of lights. A sense of, underneath, the ruins of another older river & then another & another; a depositional sequence of events. *Mille-feuille, mille-fiori*, the interleaving of crack willow & goat willow. Speckled wood, clouded yellow.

blue   blue my love: is
    blue your illuminating
            presence in my life

XI.
Tayl mose, Long-tailed Tit
(Aegithalos caudatus)
For Linda

Outside described as the colour of breath condensing on glass; the chill amnesia of fog. Instances of clarity & fading as if from radio interference. Shuttered sentences. Fur-gloved fingers of magnolia buds poke through submerged etymologiesofsuchwordsas "garden", "enclosure", "boundary wall". Interiors hollowed by absence. Cross-quarter days herald the cessation of old land-tenure agreements, the lost chartulary of the town mapped by street-lights still tied to winter circuits. The inclusion, here, of a "decorative motif" enlivens the depopulated margins of the written page. A series of short, restless surges, inverted landings in the leafless branches of the Judas tree; Jack-in-the-Bottle, bottle tit, bum barrel. Hedge mumruffin. Elsewhere in time, conversation alights on the two thousand six hundred feathers lining the nest; additions or subtractions made by researchers prompting immediate readjustments in favour of the preferred number. Dichotomies occur between the elaborated shapes of speech & an unarticulated persistence of the image within neural connections to perceived shifts in cloud strata. A moment of absolution among the accessories of horticulture; moisture droplets ringing the patrimonial bird-bath. Cursory insectivorous questing. Scarlet eyelid-wattles.

                    recall of tiny
                    doll-sized memory   upswing
                                of an empty branch

XII.
Vuelduare, Fieldfare
(Turdus pilaris)
for Nick H.

Wing to me enough, harsh thing & wakeful; a tethering of the migration loop. Feathers are brisk, they are impervious, scintillate. The Big Felty, nubbed with jostling quills. Out of a dirty sky; air full of it (whatever it is), grainy like semolina, coupled with severe hypoglycaemic episodes. Grips harder, applies torque. Treads of the ice-tractor; *fimbulvetr*, the ending of days. Ranging the fields' white miscellany, statements constructed from glass in a majuscule hand, the sharpness of hooked minims. "Little blocky feet". Flight-patterns cut white white white the scuts of three roe deer as they disappear down into darkness, rim-lit. Dark scar of subsequent waters, a sourceless chuckling; interpolation of loanwords & alien kennings within local narratives. In the wake of their hellion gods, sleek flotillas perform daylight raids on garden pyracantha. Trading of playful insults, soft incursions into relict orchards, *vapnatak*, a symbolic flourish confirms the decisions of those assembled. Stellar-frozen umbelliferae; pruina, loosely deposited. Transfers between ash trees, crown to crown. Leaves daubings of fruity excrement.

gorged
among Golden Hornet apples
I love you

rotten

XIII.

Fesaunt, Pheasant
(Phasianus colchicus)

A needle does not yet exist to drill these bone-ends for threading; this amulet in remembrance of the dead. Pain accepted as an explication of growth, slivers & thorns a means of securing paper-thin sections of secondary calligraphy, wetly unfolding. In leaves of hedge-maple. Flesh stutters & fails, allows ingress. Violets take root within a lattice of barbules, elegant self-assemblages of optical nanostructures. Light: as a feather. Remiges & rectrices. She waits by the blood in silence, welded to a complex geology, the inclusive hills. Dark Lane, Pink Knoll Hollow, Horse Scratch Field, everywhere a map for somewhere else, textually enriched by silts & marls, pleistocene clays. Pollarded, the countryside engineered to near riot; stirred for a bird, the lie of the land. Lawless laws. A socket, enucleate; splanchnic cavity plangent as the recess of an ancient rebec. Tersely set aside. The spurred feet of a fallen crusader, *deo non fortuna*. At the foot of the page, three kings pursue their journey through a delicate landscape occupied by a dog hunting a hare. Celandine pollen, caught in the creases of the *herepath*, the military road.

> gules, a cross
> argent & crosier in pale
> or debruised

XIV.
Larke, Skylark
(Alauda arvensis)
for Luke

Was once animal. Weight of a new-born calf, living inks perfused throughout its skin. *Mirabile dictu.* In winter season, the wether being not to owtragios, dothe waxe wonderus fatte. Sprung out from under this weight of words, the great singing heart tore right out of it, pinned against sky. Turning a blind eye to. Sumped in ranunculus, claws of clutched light. Fugitive moments of response amongst predators & prey leave stigmata on flesh, on instinct. Quiet, quiet. Occluded memories of feint & double-bluff nest unharmed within celebrations for decayed fallstreaks of ice, hypothetically plotted. Cirrus intortus. At the perihelion, light bleeds into black, darkness widens under sparkle of whatever joy. Head over heels, nothing holds but in small things, enshrined in nitrogen, agricultural dust. Imbricate; the overlapping of leaves, of roof-tiles, a late the Abbate of Shirburne maner place, boundaries endorsed by badger latrines. Rumours of ancient deerparks recede into mythic dissolve, a "dry & sinuous valley", a king's grace invested in soil. Messaging via the contraplex: *someone told me it was #fossilfriday @ dawn how do you sing a cluster on #dictionaryofstone.* Profuse, unpremeditated, delivered soaring. Released unto the day. Echo, echo lalia la la la

           from yesterday's footprint, a
              seed   sprouts pale,

                  cotelydonous

XV.
Cormerant, Cormorant
(Phalacrocorax carbo)
for Kim B. Ashton

To kick off one's shoes and throw them. Slipping between pleated histories at the lake's surface, brilliant or dazzling, the *coup de foudre*. Fortunately falling folded amongst these structures of unmaking, these collusions in perceptual paradox. Stunned by the flashover irrupting capillary walls in arborescent erythema; keraunographic markings reveal the pathologies of lightning, a dermal feathering. To covet the silk of your downpourings; calculations in drowning, weighed down by little stones: *I have called you by name, you are mine, when you pass through the waters I will be with you.* Breathing our stories into each other's mouths, reaffirming mutual tales of origin. Stuck in the craw. Bloodlines drawn across the lawns; a thumbnail splitting the stems of genealogical daisy-chains, she's reading for the part of kate in the shrew (o mother); a screwing down of migrainous clouds, spreading stain of strawberry ice. Time's passage in fond, undigested lumps. A hem of bindweed, woundwort & pendulous sedge, stitched into. Lap of a wave to the hand, and. No less liquid than.

          black rainbow dive: mercurial
            bubbles escape the murder-beak, dark
                          mucoid throat

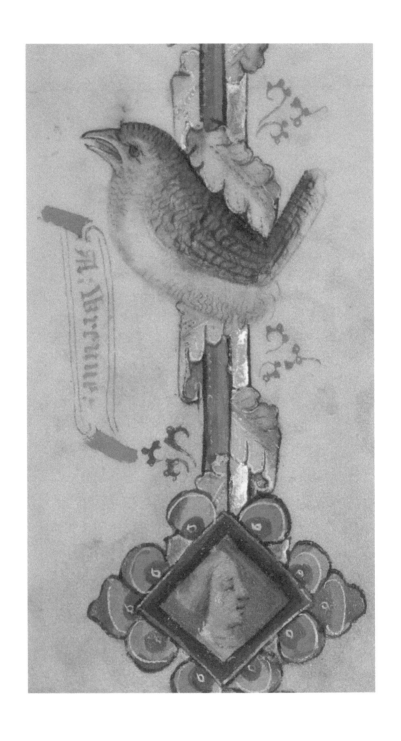

XVI.
Wrenne, Wren
(Troglodytes troglodytes)
for Chris T.

Slightly curved downwards, faintly marked wavy, narrow
bars of wavy darker indistinctly spotted amongst wreckage.
Rump reddish. Crevices & holes of rock, sprouting, lopped.
Nimrod being lost in Orion & Osyris in the Doggestarre,
within accidental collections of dead leaves, leaf-corbels.
Four-fold equations of cryptic perspectives through;
studded, fallen, scrolled off the wall of banded wavy.
Ladymasse, lullen, luvely. Russeting surrounds a deep stem
basin, depository of song. Resounds & cries out against.
Epicuticular wax particles embedded, rephrasing the
static of stretched light over wavy bars of ridge & furrow.
White slipped medieval tiles. Brought down by sticks &
stones, forks & knives; an arrow's insert between leg bone
& tendon. By the year's wheel turning to manifold trickles.
Legacies of overnight cloud, cyclone Eva unwinding the
water's chains. Wroth silver pays homage to the branched
god, resplendent in deciduous velvet, *commyth agayne
from dethh to lyff in his whyght skynne.* Trifoliate cusping
& radiant outward in problematic scratches, deeply;
though he be little, deeply reinscribed. Cutty, close-sitter,
jarring jubilous.

           dark sparkles through
               tracery with small angelic
                   reset

                       fragments

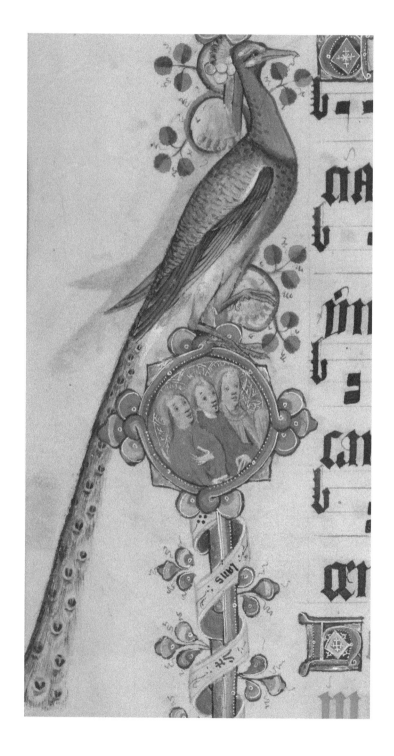

XVII.
Unnamed, identified as Peacock
(Pavo cristatus)
for Steve Batty

Our gorse commons lie neglected & abandoned, a forgotten artefact of our cultural history.

A purse of land, coarsely woven. This certain waste of ffurzies & other fewell; a chafed place & barren, lying in the broad comon. Scar tissue knotting together, seared, scalloped, scythed, serrated. Invariably furrowed & stiff. Patterns of transhumance reassert themselves through use-names inscribed upon the maps; summoned by walking, in deep-trodden utterance. Outlying manorial, cut loose from memory, coterminous with the economy of its lexicon. Venomous catabolism of fractured shadows at the selvedge: *shakeshakeshake* so shwanky down Hethfeldstrete, turning out the toes among spoil-heaps and gravel (the foulest feet & rivelled), the Tarshishim, the brilliant one. A pavement of stately dance. Curator of moldewarp archaeology, the mute ostrakon. Areareth up, off the hizzle. Colours like noisy fire of leaves in the wind, palpable stains, turning inside the flask; *distillatio.* At the threshold of wakening, strikes at the heart. Random promises of knightly violence in a shaffe of pakok-fedird arrows. *Tokeii tukkiyim.* Screaming against the storm, the domination of black. Papilionaceous, myrmechochorus. Sodden with honey, it cleareth the mouth.

for he hath an horrible voice:

voice of a fiend
head of a serpent
pace of a thief

XVIII.
Mose Cok, Great tit
(Parus major)
for Frances Hatch

Crushed eggshell, calcinated bird bones produce a patina of white, shimmer through dimpse. Oak iron-gall gnaws the skin's surface the knife-tip holds taut, bisecting the cranium to a rush of wings, inhuman hungers of feathers & blood. Salmortis. Surrounding a whitish spot, tipped with white, edged with light, tinged; the umbellule, ribbed & floating amid the floral envelope. *Hulver, hedge-rife, star-wort, witch wiggin, mother-die.* And divided longitudinally somewhat carelessly put together white in ground-colour, spotted & freckled, of varied intensity; imprimature of the zygote. A song-thread pulled from the verdure tapestry, finely twisted. Dense, tangled. A multiplicity of doors. Beyond childish repetitions: abandoned twigloos, rings of ash, shift & settle into a nameless forgetting. Green flaxlands, ploughed flaxlands, unravelling, bordering between the remembered & the real; a hollow gate-post choking with mast. Cotton weft fibrils in constructions of running water; overshot foaming white of inflexed petals. *Cramp bark, staunchweed, mouse-ear, scabby-may, hagthorn.* Fallen on stone. Tree-babbler, bidding this ripple of woodland from the textual river; weaving, unwoven. Bee-biter, pickcheese.

          from hell to heaven
     rounding the round world   dropping
               a stone through

XIX.
Wodewale, Green Woodpecker
(Picus viridis)
in memory of A. B. Bletsoe

Chips & bits, glittering, gritted. A regular split-fig; goes where the devil can't & that's between the oak & the rind. *Shalt feed off stuff betwixt bark & bole, shalt never drink save when it rains.* Pan-daemonium hatched from a piciform egg, lucifer rising. Surprising yellow. Northern meanderly blocking hot blocks of air, increasing shear under outbreaks of saharan dust albedo & volcanic aerosol underpins oceanic multidecadal oscillations. Protrusible & sticky. Sentinel woods cohere around a collapsed orchard nucleus. Leaf-scorch, needle cast; disease a message in the body text, bleeding canker micromoth incursive, black walnut nourished from emanations of the gathered dead. Inserted into the calyx throat; rose-purple, slightly notched with small & distant horny teeth, glaucous beneath. Dehiscent, drifting; smoothly white plumed. Pollen grains, the empty snail-spiral, drystone walling, bound together by lichen & wevet, fluctuant intra marginals. Travelled times before; land of the *folke,* accelerated migratory shifts push into untimely unsettle-ments of being. *There's an awful lot of blue sky left in this isn't there?* Antiphone as ornithography. Upright jizz, clumsily hopping. *Come on & rest now.*

into the trees crying *pleu*
pleu pleu pleu rain
foul wet tile wood
spate

XX.
Wop cok, male Bullfinch, misidentified as Wop hen
(Pyrrhula pyrrhula)

Sometimes a little wool, hair, or a few feathers. Thick, quick-set in hedges or rough with scattered clumps & underlying blotches; plum bird, lum budder. That devoureth the blowthe of fruit. Muting & fluted retrieval of sequences from the inner cochlea of memory modules synchronously & strongly ululant, consecutive. Short & deep shiny black prominent, in soft unripened state. Maintaining a low profile. Nipped off, crushed, rolled around the tongue, discarded into wildings; a marmulate of cherries mingled with juice of rasps & red currants, floribunda. Pulviplume ghosting of birdstrike on glass. Things once loved are now betrayed, cradled in absence; transition walls, projected on a ground of darker politics, still bear vestiges *(carpel, petiole, stipule)*. One prick to the ball & the vision is lost, weaverlands falling to shadow; east field, the butts, twelve-acre lane. Lilac fascia, iliac fossa. A pleasing fullness of belly, small fire like a stored pear; the finch the flame, how far can its light carry, smoke bent over the spring allotments. Borrowed radiance in recollection, intrinsic, mainlining straight down into earth, root-deep, crocked. Peradventure, to keep all year, there may be requisite a little more sugar.

> all the joly briddes smale do
> > change their song & each moment lustrous
> > white

LOCATIONS

ACKNOWLEDGEMENTS

Several of the poems have appeared in the following publications and forms:

I-IX *Landscape from a Dream*, by Elisabeth Bletsoe
(Shearsman Books, Exeter, 2008)

I-IX *Infinite Difference: Other Poetries by UK Women Poets*,
ed. Carrie Etter (Shearsman Books, Exeter, 2010)

XI *The Ground Aslant: An Anthology of Radical Landscape
Poetry*, ed. Harriet Tarlo (Shearsman Books, Exeter, 2011)

X-XIII *LPB Micro #6*, illustrated by Frances Hatch, produced
by Steven Hitchins, 2013

X, XII, XIV, XVI *The Lonely Crowd 7*, guest poetry editor
Chris Cornwell

XIII *Molly Bloom 10*, ed. Aidan Semmens

I, VIII *Ornithology*, composed by Kim B. Ashton, piano
Clare Hammond

XV, XVII, XVIII *The Fortnightly Review 06/2018*, poetry editor
Peter Riley

XIX, XX *Molly Bloom 24*, edited by Aidan Semmens.

9 781848 617483